W9-AQO-878

Uniquely
Oregon

Mary Boone

Heinemann Library
Chicago, Illinois

© 2004 Heinemann Library
a division of Reed Elsevier Inc.
Chicago, Illinois

Customer Service 888-454-2279

Visit our website at www.heinemannlibrary.com

All rights reserved. No part of this publication
may be reproduced or transmitted in any form or
by any means, electronic or mechanical, including
photocopying, recording, taping, or any
information storage and retrieval system, without
permission in writing from the publisher.

Designed by Heinemann Library
Printed in China by WKT Company Limited.

08 07 06 05 04
10 9 8 7 6 5 4 3 2 1

**Library of Congress
Cataloging-in-Publication Data**

Boone, Mary, 1963–
    Uniquely Oregon / Mary Boone.
        p. cm. -- (Heinemann state studies)
Includes bibliographical references and index.
    ISBN 1-4034-4659-8 (lib. bdg.) --
    ISBN 1-4034-4728-4 (pbk.)
    1. Oregon -- Juvenile literature. [1. Oregon.]
I. Title. II. Series.
    F876.3.B66 2004
    979.5'044--dc22

                                2003025725

Cover Pictures

Top (left to right) State capitol, Native
Americans at powwow, state flag, Cannon
Beach **Main** Crater Lake

Acknowledgments
Development and photo research by
Book Builders LLC

The author and publishers are grateful to the
following for permission to reproduce copyrighted
material:

Cover photographs by (top, L-R) Doug Wilson/
Corbis; Bohemian Nomad Picturemakers/Corbis;
Joe Sohm/Alamy Images; Bill Ross/Corbis; (main)
Galen Rowell/Corbis.

Cover photographs by (top, L–R): Doug
Wilson/Corbis; Bohemian Nomad
Picturemakers/Corbis; Joe Sohm/Alamy; Bill
Ross/Corbis; (main): Galen Rowell/Corbis

Title page (L-R): David R. Frazier Photolibrary/
Alamy; George and Montserrate Schwartz/Alamy;
Steven Holt/Stockpix. Contents page: USFWS. p.5
Courtesy Sally McAleer; p. 6 Bill Ross/Corbis; p. 7
NCTC Image Library/USFWS; p. 8, 14T, 16T, 26T,
26B Steven Holt/Stockpix; p. 9, 42, 45 IMA for
Book Builders LLC; p.10 David R. Frazier
Photolibrary/Alamy; p. 12 Charles Cangialosi/
Alamy; p. 13T Joe Sohm/Alamy; p. 13B One Mile
Up; p. 14, 15M, 15B, 17B USFWS; p. 16M Tom
Boyden/eNature; p. 16B, 17T Courtesy Oregon
Bluebook; p. 18, 20 Culver; p. 19 Jill Ergenbright;
p. 22T Culver; p. 22B AP Photo; p. 23 Courtesy
Bookstrap Institute; p. 24T Douglas Kirkland/
Corbis; p. 24B Photo by Mark A. Philbrick/BYU;
p. 25 George and Montserrate J. Schwartz/Alamy;
p. 27 Doug Wilson/Corbis; p. 28 Courtesy Salem
Convention and Visitors Association; p. 31
Bohemian Nomad Picturemakers/Corbis; p. 32
Courtesy Portland Guadalajara Sisters City
Association; p. 33 Courtesy Hazelnut Marketing
Board; p. 34 Lisa Koenig/Stockfood America; p. 36
Galen Rowell/Corbis; p. 37, 38B Rick Bowmer/AP
Photo; p. 38T Dave Nishitani/OSU; p. 39 USDA
Forest Service; p. 40 Corbis; p. 41 Courtesy
Timberline Lodge; p. 42 Monserrate J. Schwartz;
p. 44 Brad Mitchell/Alamy.

Special thanks to Marilyn Couture, formerly of the
Department of Anthropology, Linfield College,
McMinnville, Oregon, for her expert comments in
the preparation of this book.

Every effort has been made to contact copyright
holders of any material reproduced in this book.
Any omissions will be rectified in subsequent

Some words are shown in bold, **like this.**
You can find out what they mean by looking
in the glossary.

Contents

SHERWOOD BRANCH LIBRARY
APR - 4 2006

Uniquely Oregon

Oregon is unique. It is a "one of a kind" place. For example, Oregon is the nation's leading provider of lumber. Forests cover nearly half the state. Oregon also contains both some of the wettest and driest places in the United States. This book will help you understand these and many other things that make Oregon unique.

ORIGIN OF THE STATE'S NAME

No one is certain how Oregon got its name. Many historians believe that it comes from the French word *ouragan,* which means hurricane or storm. It was the name the French gave to the rugged and wild Columbia River, which forms part of the state's northern border.

MAJOR CITIES

Oregon is home to 3.5 million people. About 2.4 million, or 67 percent, of those residents live in cities and towns.

Salem is Oregon's capital and, with 136,924 residents, is the state's third-largest city. It is located in the Willamette Valley, along the banks of the Willamette River. The city is surrounded by vineyards and farms that produce crops including wheat, vegetables, fruits, flowers, herbs, nuts, and Christmas trees. Salem is home to Willamette University, the first university established in the West. In 1877 it became one of the first colleges in the country to admit both men and women.

Portland, known as the City of Roses because of the many parks that dominate its landscape, is Oregon's largest city with a population of 529,121. It is located about 70 miles from the Pacific Ocean, where the Columbia River meets the Willamette River. Thousands of ships travel in and out of the Port of Portland each day. Many of those ships carry automobiles into the United States. The Port of Portland is not only the number one auto port on the West Coast, it is also the third busiest auto port in the country. Portland is home to 240 parks, ranging in size from the 5,090-acre Forest Park to Mills End Park, the nation's smallest park at just 452 square inches.

Home to 137,893 people, Eugene is Oregon's second-largest city. The Willamette River runs through the heart of the city and the McKenzie River joins the Willamette just north of town. Eugene is located in Lane County, which produces more timber than any other county in Oregon. The city is home to the University of Oregon, Northwest Christian College, Lane Community College, and Eugene Bible College.

Eugene often is referred to as the "Emerald City" because of the forest that borders three sides of the city.

Oregon's Geography and Climate

Oregon is located along the Pacific Ocean north of California and south of Washington. Oregon is divided from north to south by the Cascade Mountains. The ocean and the mountains shape both the land and the **climate.**

LAND

Oregon's land can be divided into six main regions: the Coastal region, Willamette lowlands, Cascade Mountains, Klamath Mountains, Columbia plateau, and Basin and Range region.

Cannon Beach, in northwest Oregon, is home to Haystack Rock, a 235-foot-tall freestanding rock, or monolith. It is the world's third-largest coastal monolith.

The Coastal region is a strip of land less than 25 miles wide that runs the length of the state between the Pacific Ocean and

the Coast Mountains. The region consists of 400 miles of beaches and low mountains covered with forests of spruce, fir, and hemlock.

The Willamette lowlands are east of the Coastal region and west of the Cascade Mountains. This is the most varied of Oregon's agricultural regions, producing crops including vegetables, berries, hazelnuts, hops, and **nursery products.**

The Cascade Mountains are the only active volcanic chain south of Alaska. The Cascades include more than a dozen large **volcanoes,** including Mt. Hood, the highest mountain in the state at 11,239 feet above sea level. This region is also home to Crater Lake. The lake lies inside a volcanic basin that was created when Mount Mazama erupted more than 7,700 years ago.

Snow is rare along Oregon's coastline but many inland locations, particularly those at higher elevations, receive plenty. In 1950, Crater Lake reported 903 inches of snow.

The Klamath Mountains are located in southwestern Oregon. Unlike most mountain ranges in North America, the Klamaths run east to west, instead of north to south. The Klamaths are rich in mineral and ore deposits including gold, copper, nickel, and platinum. The region has a diverse landscape including gentle foothills, wide flat valleys, rugged peaks, and deep canyons. The Rogue and Klamath rivers run through the region.

Oregon's High Desert region contains more than 13.4 million acres of public land that can be used by all citizens.

The Columbia plateau is rugged and dry. It also is known as Oregon's High Desert country. The region covers the eastern two-thirds of the state. Desert plants including bunch grass and sage brush provide shelter to rabbits and lizards. There are few trees and little surface water. The topsoil, created by volcanic ash from ancient Cascade Mountain eruptions, is more than 100 feet thick. The region's low mountains, including the Blue, Wallowa, and Ochoco ranges, are dotted with pines, firs, and low-growing juniper trees. Hells **Canyon,** the deepest river **gorge** in North America, is located in this region.

The Basin and Range region covers the southeastern part of Oregon. It consists of a few steep mountains and flat valley floors. It is the only part of Oregon not formed by volcanic action. Instead, the Basin and Range region was formed when large blocks of the earth's crust tilted along fault lines, or cracks, to form mountain ranges.

CLIMATE

Unlike the weather, which changes day after day, climate rarely changes. It is the normal weather of a place.

There are two distinct climates within Oregon. The western part of the state is wetter and milder than eastern Oregon. Across the state, places that have a high **elevation** are often colder and wetter than lowlands.

Oregon's monthly average temperatures range greatly. Ontario, located along the Idaho border, is one of the state's hot spots; its monthly high temperature in July is 95°F. Enterprise, in northeastern Oregon, is one of the state's coldest places. Enterprise's average high temperature in December is 31°F. The highest temperature ever recorded in Oregon is 119°F, on July 11, 1898, at Prineville and August 10, 1898, at Pendleton. The state's lowest temperature, -54°F, was recorded on February 9, 1933, at Ukiah and February 10, 1933, at Seneca. In 1989, Seneca had a weeklong cold spell, when the average low temperature was more than -40°F.

Most western Oregon locations tend to receive the bulk of their annual precipitation from November to March. East of the Cascades, precipitation is more evenly divided throughout the year.

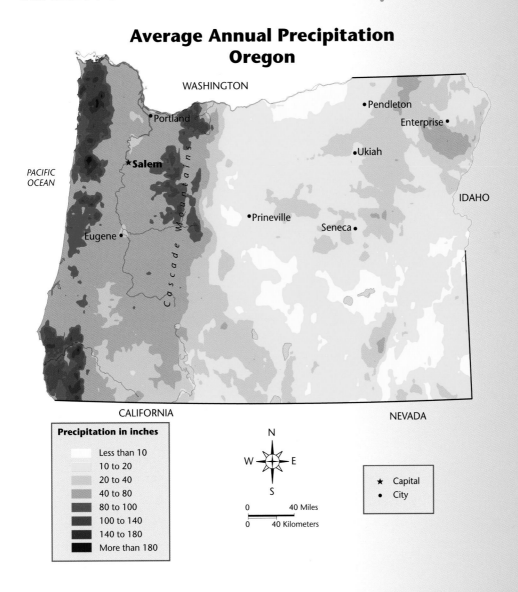

Average Annual Precipitation
Oregon

WASHINGTON

•Pendleton

Enterprise •

•Portland

•Ukiah

★Salem

PACIFIC
OCEAN

IDAHO

Cascade Mountains

•Prineville

Seneca •

Eugene •

CALIFORNIA

NEVADA

Precipitation in inches

Less than 10
10 to 20
20 to 40
40 to 80
80 to 100
100 to 140
140 to 180
More than 180

N
W—✦—E
S

0   40 Miles
0   40 Kilometers

★ Capital
• City

Famous Firsts

NATURAL WONDERS

Hells **Canyon** is the deepest river **gorge** in North America. It is located along the Snake River in both Idaho and Oregon. The canyon walls are more than 7,900 feet deep in places. That is more than 1.3 miles! By comparison, the Grand Canyon is only 6,250 feet deep. The enormous depth of Hells Canyon results in extremes in temperature. In the summer, the temperature at the river often reaches 110°F. At the canyon's highest elevations, it is common to find as much as five feet of snow in June.

Hells Canyon is located within the 652,488-acre Hells Canyon National Recreation Area.

Crater Lake, located in southwestern Oregon, is the deepest lake in the United States and the seventh-deepest in the world. Measuring 1,932 feet deep, the lake was formed about 7,700 years ago when the tip of a volcano now known as Mount Mazama collapsed. Lava flows sealed the bottom of the basin, allowing it to fill with 4.6 trillion gallons of water from rainfall and snow melt. That is enough water to fill more than five million Olympic-size swimming pools. In 1902, President Theodore Roosevelt signed a bill making Crater Lake and the surrounding 183,224 acres a national park.

Crater Lake National Park is the country's fifth oldest national park.

Sea Lion Caves, located eleven miles north of Florence on the Pacific coast, is the world's largest sea cave. A sea cave is formed by waves pounding against a cliff. In 1880, Oregon ship captain William Cox became the first European to find the 25 million-year-old cave. The cave was opened to visitors in 1932; the same three families who opened the cave still own and run it. The 2-acre cave is home to around 200 stellar sea lions. Unlike other types of sea lions, stellar sea lions have external ear flaps and flippers that point forward. Visitors can take a 208-foot elevator-ride into the stadium-sized natural cavern where they can watch the sea lions swim and rest on rocky ledges.

BIG, BIGGER, BIGGEST

Oregon State University in Corvallis is home to the world's largest tsunami research lab. A tsunami is an enormous wave—often 150 feet tall—caused by an earthquake or volcano under the ocean. In 2003, scientists at the lab began using simulators—machines that make models of tsunamis. The scientists study the models to better understand the massive waves in order to help people who live in tsunami-prone regions prepare for them. Since 1945, 6 tsunamis have killed more than 350 people and caused $500 million worth of damage in Hawaii, Alaska, and along the West Coast of the United States.

The H.J. Andrews Experimental Forest, established in 1948 and located 90 miles southwest of Bend, is one of the nation's largest research centers dedicated to studying environment and **ecology.** Experiments in the 15,800-acre forest provide important information about climate, stream flow, and water quality. More than 2,500

Harbor seals are the real stars at Seaside Aquarium. They routinely clap, splash, and bark to earn praise and treats from visitors.

people visit the forest each year to participate in research or other educational activities.

IMPORTANT DEVELOPMENTS

Seaside Aquarium was the first facility in the world to successfully breed harbor seals. The privately owned aquarium was established in 1937 and is one of the oldest on the West Coast.

Oregon State **entomologist** Robert L. Goulding developed the world's first flea collars for dogs and cats in 1960. Before that time, pet owners could only treat fleas with powders, sprays, and soaps.

Portland is home to the world's first alien studies museum. The Portland Alien Museum, which opened in 2003, is a serious international research center designed to learn more about those who say they have seen or been abducted by aliens. Research conducted at the museum is designed to help understand things such as sightings of Unidentified Flying Objects (UFOs) and human abductions.

Oregon's State Symbols

The 33 stars on Oregon's flag symbolize that Oregon was the 33rd state admitted to the Union.

OREGON STATE FLAG

Oregon has the only state flag with different pictures on each side. A portion of the state seal appears on one side, and a beaver standing on its dam is on the reverse side. The beaver is a reminder of the state's early fur-trapping days. The flag was adopted in 1925.

OREGON STATE SEAL

Harvey Gordon designed the Oregon state seal. The legislature adopted it in 1858. A departing ship on the seal signifies the end of British influence in Oregon and an arriving ship represents the rise of U.S. power.

STATE MOTTO: SHE FLIES WITH HER OWN WINGS

"She Flies With Her Own Wings" was first adopted as Oregon's motto in 1854—long before statehood. The motto reflected the desire of settlers in **Oregon Country** to form their own government, separate from both Great Britain and the United States.

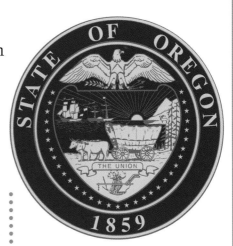

The state seal's covered wagon and team of oxen represent the pioneers who settled the state.

"Oregon, My Oregon"

Land of the Empire Builders, Land of the
Golden West;
Conquered and held by free men, Fairest
and the best.
Onward and upward ever, Forward and on,
and on;
Hail to thee, Land of Heroes, My Oregon.

Land of the rose and sunshine, Land of the
summer's breeze;
Laden with health and vigor, Fresh from the
western seas.
Blest by the blood of **martyrs,** Land of the
setting sun;
Hail to thee, Land of Promise, My Oregon.

In 1957, state lawmakers changed the motto to "The Union" to commemorate the idea that the country could not be divided. In 1987, legislators voted to return to the original motto to honor the state's independent spirit.

STATE NICKNAME: THE BEAVER STATE

Oregon is called the Beaver State because the animal's fur was important to early settlers and hunters.

STATE SONG: "OREGON, MY OREGON"

Lyricist J.A. Buchanan of Astoria and composer Henry B. Murtagh of Portland created "Oregon, My Oregon" in 1920. Their song won a contest sponsored by the Society of Oregon Composers and became the state song in 1927.

STATE FLOWER: OREGON GRAPE

State lawmakers named the Oregon grape the state flower in 1899. It is a low-growing plant that is some-

The Oregon grape has yellow flowers in early summer and dark blue berries that ripen in fall.

what misnamed because it produces berries not grapes. The plant is native to Oregon.

Douglas fir trees grow to an average height of 200 feet and can be found throughout western Oregon. It is one of the most popular species of Christmas trees.

STATE TREE: DOUGLAS FIR

Oregon chose the Douglas fir as its state tree in 1939. About three-fourths of the forests in western Oregon are made of Douglas fir. Its wood is used in hundreds of products from **plywood** and utility poles to paper towels.

STATE BIRD: WESTERN MEADOWLARK

Schoolchildren in a 1927 poll sponsored by the Oregon Audubon Society chose the western meadowlark as the state bird. It is native to Oregon and has a distinctive warbling whistle.

Meadowlarks make their nests on the ground and lay three to seven eggs, which are white with brown and purple spots.

STATE FISH: CHINOOK SALMON

In 1961, the Oregon legislature named the Chinook salmon the state fish. It is the largest of the Pacific salmons and is native to Oregon's river basins.

Most Chinook salmon found in Oregon rivers weigh 18 to 22 pounds. The largest Chinook ever caught was hooked in 1949 and weighed 126 pounds.

TRABLAH HOARBE GRITT

The American beaver's wide, flat tail acts as a steering device while swimming, a prop for standing upright, a lever when dragging tree logs, and a noise maker when it is slapped on the water.

STATE ANIMAL: AMERICAN BEAVER

Oregon named the American beaver the state animal in 1969. Prized for its fur, the beaver was over trapped by early settlers and became scarce. Thanks to breeding programs, beaver once again populate the state's waterways.

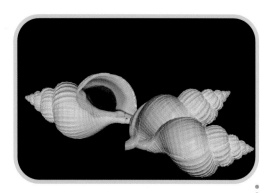

The shell of the Oregon hairy triton is the largest of Oregon seashells, creatures, reaching lengths of up to five inches.

STATE SEASHELL: OREGON HAIRY TRITON

In 1989, the state made the Oregon hairy triton's shell its state seashell. The shell gets its name because it is covered with rows of brown bristles. The hairy triton can be found along Oregon's beaches.

STATE GEMSTONE: SUNSTONE

Sunstone became the Oregon state gemstone in 1987. There are many varieties of sunstone in the world, ranging in color from yellow and pink to green and red. The Oregon sunstone is unique because it contains copper flakes that make it glitter. Oregon sunstones are the only ones in the world of gem quality.

The sunstone is commercially mined in southeast Oregon.

STATE ROCK: THUNDEREGG

In 1965, at the request of rock collectors, the Oregon legislature named the thunderegg the state rock. On the outside, thundereggs, which range in size from one inch to five feet in diameter, look like mud balls. When cut open and polished, they look like opals, five-pointed stars, or miniature crystal gardens. Thundereggs were formed during periods of volcanic activity in Oregon and Washington about 30 million years ago.

STATE NUT: HAZELNUT

The legislature named the hazelnut, also known as the filbert, the state nut in 1989 because the state grows 99 percent of the nation's commercial crop.

STATE INSECT: OREGON SWALLOWTAIL

In 1979, state lawmakers made the Oregon swallowtail the state insect. This butterfly is at home in the lower canyons formed by the Columbia River and its **tributaries.**

Oregonians call hazelnuts filberts. Some people believe the name originally referred to Aug. 22, the feast day of Saint Philibert, the day the nuts were first harvested in England.

Swallowtails seen in the spring are generally lighter in color than those seen in late summer or fall to blend with the color of the season's plants.

Oregon's History & People

From Native American villagers to Spanish and English sailors to American fur trappers and traders, many diverse people helped form the state of Oregon.

Native American Heritage

For at least 10,000 years people have lived in what is now known as Oregon. The names these earliest people had for themselves and the languages they spoke are unknown. Their **artifacts,** including primitive spears, **pictographs,** and pottery, offer some clues about what these people ate and where they lived.

When Europeans began arriving in the region in the 1500s, they found Native Americans living throughout the area. These tribes had lifestyles as varied as the land upon

The Chetco tribe migrated to Oregon more than 2,000 years ago. They settled the southwestern portion of the state. Their descendents still live along the Chetco River.

which they lived. The native peoples of the Oregon coast and western valleys, for example, lived in a wet, forested climate that required them to build cedar homes for shelter. They fished, hunted wild game, and picked berries.

Tribes living in eastern Oregon endured more extreme weather. The tribes, including the Cayuse, Umatilla, and Nez Perce, constructed pole-frame tents for the hot summers and dug into the earth to build pit houses for protection from winter's cold and wind. They hunted deer both for the meat and hides and harvested salmon.

EARLY EXPLORERS

As early as the 1540s, Spanish and British explorers began sailing to what is now the Oregon coast in search of land and wealth. Beginning in the 1770s, many explorers headed across the North American continent to find the fabled "great river of the west." In 1775, Captain Bruno Heceta of Spain was sent to the Pacific Northwest to discourage Russian fur traders from gaining footholds along the coast. He reported seeing a large bay, but a severe storm prevented him from exploring it. In 1792, American Robert Gray noted a flow of muddy water fanning from the shore while traveling through the area. Believing this might be the river explorers were seeking, Gray crossed the sand bar and named the river after his ship, *Columbia Rediviva*.

People have lived along the Columbia River for more than 10,000 years. It is Oregon's most important waterway.

Gray's exploration of the Columbia River gave the United States a strong claim to the Oregon Country, which was later known as Oregon Territory. Because more was known about the land and access to it, American fur traders were encouraged to set up posts there. They often spent winters camped along the Columbia River.

THE LEWIS AND CLARK EXPEDITION

In 1804, Gray's explorations prompted President Thomas Jefferson to send Meriwether Lewis, his friend and former secretary, and William Clark to find a water route connecting the interior of the country to the trade routes of the Pacific.

With a team of 33 men known as the Corps of Discovery, Lewis and Clark traveled 2,000 miles west from St. Louis, Missouri, to the mouth of the Columbia River near what is now Astoria. There, on December 24, 1805, the Corps of Discovery built a camp named Fort Clatsop, in honor of the Native Americans who lived in the area. While in the region now known as Oregon, Lewis and Clark became the first Europeans to observe many animals and plants including the Columbia River chub, Oregon bobcat, and Cascade-Oregon grape.

THE OREGON TRAIL

Easterners learned about Oregon thanks to Lewis and Clark, as well as through letters from explorers and missionaries. Stories about the region's fertile land, timber, abundant salmon, and mild climate encouraged many people to move westward.

Trail ruts are still visible on the Oregon Trail. Thousands of covered wagons carved their ruts on their journey west.

Beginning in 1841 and continuing for twenty years, the Oregon Trail was the only route to the northwestern United States. The 2,170 mile-long trail began in Independence, Missouri, and ended in Oregon City. Roughly 300,000 fur traders, gold miners, missionaries, and **emigrants** followed this route on a trip that took five to seven months to complete.

Those who reached Oregon most often settled in the Willamette Valley to farm the area's fertile soil. Discoveries of gold on the coast and in eastern Oregon led to settlement of these regions as well. Much of the state was populated by Native Americans who depended upon fishing. When settlers polluted streams and killed fish, the tribes fought back. Conflicts erupted in other parts of the region for a variety of other reasons. For example, residents of Jacksonville, Canyonville, Kerbyville, and Gold Beach let their hogs run wild. The hogs ate acorns, a favorite Native American food. Miners drove the Takelma, Shasta, Chetco, Shasta Costa, Mikonotunne, Tututni, Galice Creeks, and Cow Creeks from their villages. The conflicts escalated to Native American Wars that lasted from the 1850s to the 1870s: the Rogue River, Modoc, Paiute, Bannock, and Nez Perce wars all ended with the tribes surrendering their land and moving onto reservations. Reservations are tracts of land set apart by the federal government for a special purpose, especially for use by Native American tribes.

Beginning in 1818, the Oregon Territory was jointly occupied by both the British and Americans. As time went by, both countries became increasing frustrated with the arrangement. The 1846 Oregon Treaty established a border between the British and American sections of the territory. The treaty stated that the 49th parallel would form the border of the United States and the British on the mainland. The 49th parallel became the U.S.-Canadian border when British Columbia became part of Canada. On February 14, 1859, Oregon became the 33rd state.

Whitman Massacre

In 1836, Dr. Marcus Whitman and his wife, Narcissa Prentiss, came overland with the caravans on the Oregon Trail. Their mission was to take religion to local tribes: the Walla Walla, Umatilla, Cayuse, and Nez Perce. The Whitmans established a **mission** at Fort Walla Walla on the Columbia River. The Native Americans were not interested in Whitman's religion, but they were interested in his ability to practice medicine.

By 1847, a measles breakout had reached the Northwest, and many Native Americans were dying from the disease while most of the settlers survived. Some Native Americans thought Whitman was poisoning their people. On November 29, 1847, Cayuse and Walla Walla warriors attacked the settlement, killing the Whitmans and all people in it.

After the massacre, Colonel Gilliam led an army of Oregon volunteers to search for the killers. He reached The Dalles, a mission on the Oregon Trail, on January 23, 1848. His men engaged in several small fights before reaching the Whitman mission. They stayed there for a time, but never were successful in capturing the men who had killed the Whitmans. The mission site was cleaned up and dedicated in 1897.

Linus Pauling attended the public elementary and high schools in Condon and Portland.

FAMOUS PEOPLE

Linus Pauling (1901–1994), chemist. Born in Portland, Pauling attended Oregon State College and the California Institute of Technology, where he later became a professor. He won the **Nobel Prize** in Chemistry in 1954 and the Nobel Peace Prize in 1963, becoming the only person ever to receive two unshared Nobel Prizes. Pauling made many discoveries related to the cause of

sickle-cell anemia, an explanation of how **anesthesia** works, and the power of Vitamin C in fighting off heart disease, cancer, and the common cold.

Douglas Engelbart is a member of the National Inventors Hall of Fame.

Douglas Engelbart (1925–   ), computer scientist. Born and raised on a farm near Portland, Engelbart graduated from Oregon State University and invented more than 45 things throughout his career. His work focused on computer components, online computing, and email. His most famous invention is the computer mouse. Engelbart made his first mouse in 1964 and got a patent for it in 1970. It was a wooden shell with two metal wheels. He nicknamed it "mouse" because the tail or cord came out the end.

Carl "Doc" Severinsen (1927–   ), musician. Born in Arlington, trumpet-playing Severinsen toured with some of the most popular groups of his time including the Charlie Barnet, Tommy Dorsey, and Benny Goodman bands. In 1949, he settled in New York as an NBC staff musician and joined *The Tonight Show* orchestra in 1962. He received a Grammy Award in 1987 for best jazz instrumental performance by a big band for his recording "Doc Severinsen and The Tonight Show Band: Volume I."

David Hume Kennerly (1947–   ), photographer. Kennerly's career began in Roseburg, where he published his first picture in the high school paper when he was fifteen years old. He later worked as a staff photographer for the *Oregon Journal* and then the *Portland Oregonian,* jobs that led him to a position with United Press International. Kennerly won the **Pulitzer Prize** for Feature Photography in 1972. He served as White House Photographer during the administration of President Gerald Ford and worked for magazines including *Time, Newsweek, Life,* and *George.* Kennerly is chairman of "Home of the Free," a national program that teaches middle-school students how photography is used in news reporting.

Cartoonist Matt Groening named The Simpsons *after his own family members.*

Sally Struthers (1948–), actress. Born and raised in Portland, Struthers is best known for her character Gloria Stivic, Archie Bunker's daughter in the 1970s sitcom *All in the Family*. She won two Emmys and is an ambassador for Save the Children, an international children's charity.

Matt Groening (1954–), cartoonist/writer. A Portland native, Groening worked as a chauffeur in California. Unhappy with his job, he created a comic called *Life in Hell*, which became the basis for eight books and a comic strip that runs in 250 U.S. newspapers. In 1990, Groening created *The Simpsons* for the Fox Network.

Danny Ainge (1959–), athlete. Ainge grew up in Eugene. He played for the Toronto Blue Jays from 1979 to 1981, while attending Brigham Young University. After college Ainge gave up baseball for his first love: basketball. He was selected by the Boston Celtics in the second round of the NBA draft and finished his 14-year professional basketball career with 1,002 three-pointers. Ainge coached the Phoenix Suns for three seasons. In May 2003, he was named executive director of basketball operations for the Boston Celtics.

Danny Ainge was the second player in NBA history to hit 900 three-point shots and the fourth to reach 1,000. On June 5, 1992, he tied the NBA playoff record by scoring 9 points in one overtime period vs. the Chicago Bulls.

Timber!

Almost half—28 million—of Oregon's 61.4 million acres is forested. Each year about $12.8 billion worth of forest products are harvested from the state.

THE TIMBER INDUSTRY

Timber has been shaping Oregon life for more than 150 years. Beginning in about 1850, loggers used handsaws and axes to cut trees from the state's mountainsides. Early loggers cut down trees without replanting and left open hillsides that **eroded** in the wind and rain. With the trees gone, there was no shade to keep streams cool, so salmon died. By the late 1800s, Congress passed laws to help ensure timber and other natural resources will be around for future generations.

Logging occurs throughout the state but is concentrated in the Cascade Range.

TIMBER AND WOOD PROCESSING

Over the years, some advances have been made in the way trees are harvested. On sloping ground, special machines can drive right up to trees, cut them down, and tear off their limbs. On steeper hills, loggers use chainsaws. The trees are moved to logging trucks using suspension wires that look like ski-lifts.

Loggers generally use one of two methods to harvest trees. Clear-cutting removes all the trees from an area. Douglas firs are clear-cut because fir seedlings cannot

Mills like this one process giant trees into products like paper.

thrive in the shade provided by mature trees that are still standing. Selective harvest removes just those trees of a certain size or species.

After trees are harvested, they are hauled to lumber mills. Most of Oregon's mills are located in western Oregon, near Eugene and Roseburg. Depending upon their ultimate use, logs may have their bark stripped from them or may be sawed into boards by special machines.

CONTROVERSY TODAY

Some of Oregon's trees have been standing for hundreds of years. This is known as old-growth timber. Old-growth forests are home to many animals, plants, and insects that cannot live anywhere else.

There have been many debates about the logging of old-growth forests. Loggers say protecting old-growth trees means entire forests are off-limit for harvesting, so they lose money. Logging companies replant the trees they cut. However, because some animals can only thrive in old trees and others do best in smaller trees, **environmentalists** say replanting new trees all at the same time is not the same as having a forest that includes trees of difference sizes.

Old-growth forests are defined in many ways, but they are generally thought to contain trees more than 250 years old.

Oregon's State Government

Salem is the capital of Oregon. It is the place where the state's government has its headquarters. The government of Oregon is modeled after the U.S. government. In both, power is divided among three branches: the legislative, executive, and judicial.

LEGISLATIVE BRANCH

Oregon's legislature consists two bodies: the senate, whose 30 members are elected to 4-year terms, and the House of Representatives, which has 60 members elected for 2-year terms. Each body may propose a state law but both must pass a **bill** before it is sent to the governor for approval. If the governor approves the bill, it becomes law. If the governor **vetoes** the bill, it can become law only if two-thirds of both legislative bodies vote to **override** the veto.

The legislature meets during odd-numbered years only. Although the state **constitution** does not specify how long lawmakers should meet, most sessions last approximately six months.

Oregon's capitol was destroyed in a fire in 1855. Its replacement also burned. The current capitol was dedicated in 1938.

A Progressive State

Oregon has a long history of progressive legislation—laws that give citizens more say in government. Oregon was the first state to elect U.S. senators by a vote of the people rather than a vote of the state legislature. It was also the first to distribute free voter pamphlets, allow **recall** of public officials, and require citizens across the state to register to vote. These laws were part of the Progressive Era—a time when reformers tried to expand democracy by giving ordinary people a greater say in government.

EXECUTIVE BRANCH

The executive branch enforces state laws. Oregon voters elect six statewide officials to manage the executive branch of government. These officials are the governor, secretary of state, treasurer, attorney general, commissioner of labor and industries, and superintendent of public instruction.

As the head of the executive branch, the governor makes budget recommendations to the legislature and oversees the state government. The governor, who is limited to two four-year terms, also may veto bills and appoint people to fill vacancies in state commissions or departments.

The secretary of state reports on Oregon's financial condition, manages statewide elections, and keeps records

Oregon's capital moved in 1851 from Salem to Oregon City. In 1855, the capital was moved to Corvallis, only to move back to Salem later that year.

for the legislature and state agencies. Should the governor be unable to perform his or her duties, the secretary of state becomes the acting governor.

The treasurer manages money received by the state from taxes, fees, and other sources. The attorney general is the state's lawyer in all court cases in which the state has an interest. The commissioner of labor and industries promotes a competitive workforce, protects the rights of workers, and enforces state laws relating to working conditions and terms of employment. The superintendent of public instruction heads up the Department of Education, which serves nearly 200 school districts.

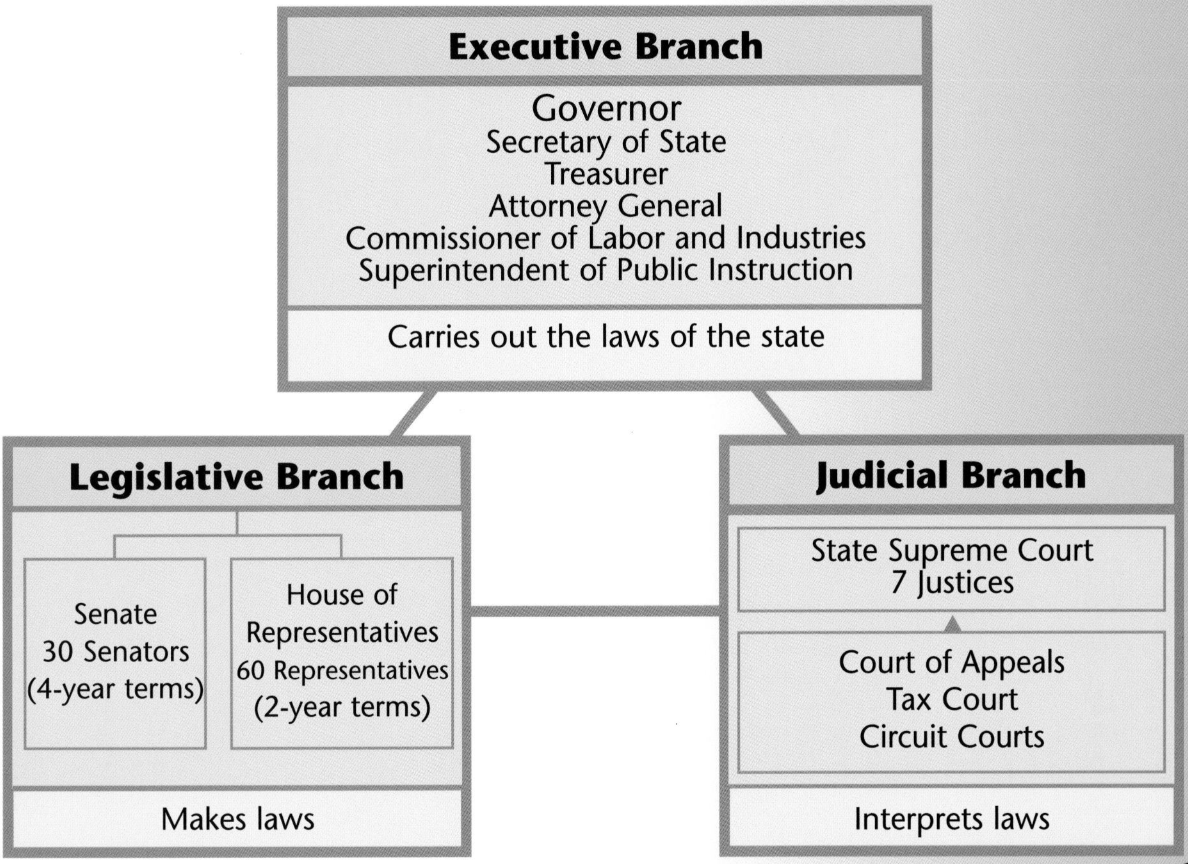

Executive Branch

Governor
Secretary of State
Treasurer
Attorney General
Commissioner of Labor and Industries
Superintendent of Public Instruction

Carries out the laws of the state

Legislative Branch

| Senate 30 Senators (4-year terms) | House of Representatives 60 Representatives (2-year terms) |

Makes laws

Judicial Branch

State Supreme Court
7 Justices

Court of Appeals
Tax Court
Circuit Courts

Interprets laws

JUDICIAL BRANCH

The judicial branch decides how state laws apply to particular cases. Oregon's circuit courts hear cases dealing with a broad range of **civil** issues including adoption, divorce, and disagreements over property. It also decides **criminal cases** such as arson, assault, and burglary. Oregon has 166 circuit judges grouped into 27 districts. Circuit court judges are elected to six-year terms.

Oregon's tax court has a **magistrate** and a regular division. Trials in the magistrate division are informal and the proceedings may be conducted by telephone or in person. Appeals from the magistrate division are made to the regular division of the tax court. Trials in the regular division are held before a judge rather than a jury.

An appeal is a request to a higher court to review and change the decision of a lower court. Oregon's court of appeals presides over all civil and criminal appeals except death-penalty cases and appeals from the tax court. Justices are elected to six-year terms.

Oregon's highest court is the state supreme court. It is composed of seven elected justices who each serve a six-year term. Members of the court elect their own chief justice. The state supreme court primarily reviews decisions of the court of appeals. When the Supreme Court decides not to review a case, the court of appeals' decision becomes final. The Oregon Supreme Court also hears direct appeals in some cases, such as those involving the death penalty, discipline of lawyers and judges, and tax court cases.

Oregon's Culture

Native Americans and people from countries around the world have settled in Oregon. Their traditions are celebrated throughout the state at annual fairs and festivals.

NATIVE AMERICAN ROOTS

About 45,200 Native Americans live in Oregon. To share their culture with others, many tribes hold celebrations called powwows. During these events, guests can join tribal members in traditional dress for drum circles, dancing, woodcarving, and beading demonstrations.

The Confederated Tribes of Umatilla's Wildhorse Powwow is one of the state's best known powwows. The celebration is held over the Fourth of July and is known for its huckleberry ice cream and Indian tacos—a dish made of **fry bread,** ground beef, green peppers, and

Today, the Umatilla people celebrate their history and culture at events like the Pendleton Roundup.

onions. Held near Pendleton, the powwow features drum and dance competitions, often drawing more than 1,000 dancers from throughout the United States. About 5,000 people attend the event each year.

Cinco de Mayo celebrations include traditional Mexican folk dances.

A BLENDING OF CULTURES

More than eight percent of Oregon's population—about 275,000 people—are **Latino.** Those who are Mexican-American celebrate the country's largest Cinco de Mayo festival, which is held in Portland each year. Cinco de Mayo, which means 5th of May, commemorates Mexico's victory over the French army at the Battle of Puebla in 1862. The celebration, which attracts 300,000 people each year, features music, a parade, dancing, and a replica Mexican village complete with shops. Vendors sell a wide variety of Mexican foods including tortillas, tamales, fajitas, and flan. The four-day event began in 1985 as a way to honor Portland's special relationship with Guadalajara, Mexico.

The state is also home to more than 100,000 Asian Americans who hold a variety of festivals that commemorate their heritage. The largest is the Oregon Asian Celebration, in Eugene. Begun in 1985, the two-day February celebration features a market, traditional dances, an art exhibit, a martial arts exhibition, and cooking demonstrations. Visitors can learn Mah Jongg, a Chinese tile-matching game, or Hanafuda, a Japanese card game. Each year the event draws about 18,000 visitors.

Oregon's Food

Oregon farmers produce wheat, cranberries, green beans, apples, nuts, and other foods. Many of the state's best-loved dishes feature ingredients grown on the state's farms or harvested from its waters.

Oregon Hazelnuts

Nearly all of the hazelnuts grown in the United States come from the rich soil of the Willamette Valley. Hazelnuts add texture and flavor to cereal, salads, entrees, and sauces.

Hazelnuts are also used in desserts like Nor'westers.

Nor'westers

Always have an adult help you when working with the oven!

1-1/2 cups sifted flour

1 teaspoon baking powder

1/4 teaspoon salt

2 tablespoons brown sugar

2/3 cup soft butter

1 cup shredded mild cheddar cheese

1 cup roasted & chopped Oregon hazelnuts

1-1/2 cups raspberry preserves

Preheat oven to 350°F. Mix flour, baking powder, salt and brown sugar. Cut butter and cheese into flour; add nuts and mix until crumbly. Grease an 8-inch square pan and spread half the mixture evenly in the pan, cover carefully with preserves and then remaining crumb mixture. Bake for 25 minutes. Cool, sprinkle with powdered sugar, and cut into bars.

Salmon has been a central part of the diets of the people of Oregon since the area was settled thousands of years ago.

SALMON AND SEAFOOD

Although the state is known for its fresh salmon, Oregon's lakes, rivers, and coastal waters hold a rich variety of seafood. An average of ten million pounds of Dungeness crab, a shellfish native to the North Pacific, are harvested in Oregon each year. The state's fishers also make impressive hauls of albacore, lingcod, rockfish, Pacific pink shrimp, Coho salmon, Northwest trout, and oysters. Oregon cooks often include fish dishes such as battered fish and chips or fish tacos in casual lunches, or crab quiche or grilled salmon steaks in elegant dinners.

OREGON BERRIES

About 85 percent of the nation's blackberries are grown in Oregon. One very tasty blackberry is the Marionberry. This berry gets its name from Marion County, the region of Oregon where it flourishes. Like other blackberries, Marionberries spoil easily, so most of them are made into jam.

Oregon's Folklore and Legends

The word *folklore* describes the stories passed from **generation** to generation. These stories entertain, tell a piece of history, teach lessons, or explain events—even if they are not always completely true. Here are some of Oregon's most popular folklore and legends.

PAUL BUNYAN'S KITCHEN

One winter, Paul Bunyan—a legendary giant lumberjack—came to log along Gimlet Creek in northeast Oregon. His kitchen was at least ten miles long and his stove was an acre long. The head cook would send four cooks to the stovetop with a side of pork tied to each of their snowshoes. They skated around, keeping the griddle greased, while eight men flipped flapjacks.

Of course, it was not just Paul Bunyan's stove that was oversized; his table was ten miles long. Young boys on bicycles rode down the middle of the table bringing food to those who needed it.

Mishaps were common that winter and one of the most memorable came when Babe the Blue Ox knocked a bag of dried peas off the counter with his tail. Those peas flew so far that they clipped the tops off nearby trees. When the peas came to rest in a hot spring, most of the crew was pleased that they had pea soup for dinner. The only ones complaining were the boys whose mothers insisted they bathe more than once a year. Those boys were angry to discover that their swimming hole had become an accidental soup pot.

WHY CRATER LAKE IS BLUE

Many Native American stories feature a coyote as the mischievous hero. This Klamath legend is one such tale.

Coyote loved to watch the stars, especially a blue star that he thought was more beautiful than the others. He noticed the blue star seemed to be close to a distant mountain.

So Coyote traveled to the mountain and climbed to the top. When the blue star appeared in the sky, he asked her to marry him. When she refused, Coyote jumped into the sky. When he tried to grab the blue star, she held him by the paws and pulled Coyote higher into the sky.

Then she dropped him. He fell so hard into the mountain that it exploded, leaving only a huge hole. As Coyote cried for his lost love, his tears filled the hole in the mountaintop, making the clear blue lake now known as Crater Lake.

Crater Lake was a place of mystery to the Klamath, who lived in the region about 7,700 years ago.

Oregon's Sports Teams

Oregonians are proud of their athletes. The Oregon Sports Hall of Fame built the Oregon Sports Museum in Portland in 1978 to share the stories of some of the state's best-known runners, basketball players, rodeo stars, and more.

PRO SPORTS

The Portland Trail Blazers entered the National Basketball Association (NBA) in 1970. The Trail Blazers were at the bottom of the standings for a few years but within seven years they became one of the league's best teams. In 1977, the Blazers won the NBA Championship. They also played in the NBA Finals against Detroit in 1990 and Chicago in 1992. Many of the sport's best players have played for the Trail Blazers over the years, including Bill Walton (1974–1979) and Clyde Drexler (1983–1995).

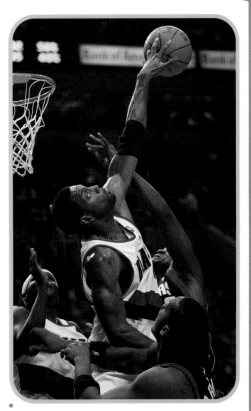

From 1982 to 2003, the Portland Trailblazers made the NBA playoffs 21 consecutive times.

COLLEGE TEAMS

Oregon State University (OSU) is located in Corvallis. Its sports teams are called the Beavers. OSU's men's basketball team has the twelfth-best record of all Division One teams in the country. Gary Payton, who has played for the NBA's Seattle Supersonics, Milwaukee Bucks, and Los Angeles Lakers, is OSU's all-time leading scorer with 2,172

OSU and UO are sports rivals. Whenever teams from the two universities compete, the match-up is called the Civil War.

points. He also holds the OSU single game scoring record of 58 points, logged against USC in 1990.

The University of Oregon (UO) is located in Eugene and plays in the Pac-10 Athletic Conference. The OU Ducks football team's most recent conference championships came in 1994, 1995, 2000, and 2001. The men's basketball team won the conference championship in 2002 and the Pac-10 Tournament in 2003. The women's basketball team won league championships in 1999 and 2000. Two recent UO athletes now playing in the pros are Detroit Lions quarterback Joey Harrington and Seattle Supersonics guard Luke Ridnour.

Steve Prefontaine

Track star Steve Prefontaine attended the University of Oregon and became the first athlete ever to win four straight college championships in the 5,000 meters. A Coos Bay native, he was a member of the 1972 U.S. Olympic team and by 1975 held the U.S. record in every track event from 2,000 to 10,000 meters. In addition to his outstanding athletic performances, he was admired for his enthusiasm and determination. Prefontaine died in a car crash in 1975 when he was just 24. Two movies—1997's *Prefontaine* and 1998's *Without Limits*—and two documentaries about his life have been made. His memory lives on in the many running trails, track meets, and memorials throughout Oregon that are named in his honor.

Oregon's Businesses and Products

Many of Oregon's industries rely on the state's natural resources, mainly farmland, timber, and fish. Tourism also depends on the state's natural resources. Many visitors come to the state to see its canyons, lakes, and mountains.

FARM PRODUCTS

Agriculture is a leading Oregon industry, with annual farm and ranch sales of about $3.5 billion. **Nursery products** are the state's number one commodity, with annual sales of $492 million. Hay is number two with sales of $363 million. Oregon leads the nation in the production of Christmas trees, grass seed, hazelnuts, peppermint, raspberries, blackberries, loganberries, and other berry crops.

Oregon's Christmas tree growers sell about 6 million trees worldwide each year.

Approximately 140,000 Oregon jobs are tied to agriculture. About 80 percent of Oregon's agricultural products are shipped out of the state or overseas. Oregon's major agriculture exports are soft white wheat, frozen French fries, grass seed, hay, and processed corn.

FISHING

Commercial fishing was one of Oregon's first industries and it is still important to the state economy. Each year about 250 million pounds of fish are caught in Oregon waters. The harvesting and processing of these fish generates about $147 million. Fewer than 200 commercial fishers work in the state but about 5,100 people work in

Nike

Nike is one of the world's best-known companies. It got its start in 1963, when Oregon University alumni and runner Phil Knight started selling Japanese-made Tiger running shoes from the trunk of his car. He called his business Blue Ribbon Sports.

Knight soon joined forces with his former coach Bill Bowerman, who began experimenting with new sole designs by pouring a liquid rubber compound into his waffle iron. Steve Prefontaine, the first major track athlete to wear Nike products, offered input about the design of the company's running shoes. Blue Ribbon Sports was renamed Nike in 1972, after the Greek goddess of victory.

Nike's world headquarters are located in Beaverton. Today, the company has 22,000 employees worldwide; 6,000 of them are based in Oregon. In 2002 Nike sold $9.9 billion worth of shoes, apparel, and other goods, making it the largest sports and fitness company in the world.

support positions, processing or transporting fish, or operating and repairing fishing vessels. Commercially, the state is known for its quantity and quality of Chinook and Coho salmon, rockfish, sole, sablefish, Pacific whiting, Dungeness crab, pink shrimp, and albacore tuna.

TOURISM

Oregon's tourism industry brings in $6.2 billion each year and provides the state with about 94,500 jobs.

The state's natural environment is one of its biggest draws. Columbia River Gorge, Crater Lake, Hells Canyon, Fort Rock, and Smith Rock are among tourists' favorite natural attractions. Oregon also boasts a number of popular human-made attractions including the Oregon Coast Aquarium, Oregon Museum of Science and Industry, Evergreen Museum of Aviation, and the End of the Oregon Trail Interpretive Center. Visitors also are drawn to Oregon's 48 covered bridges, 9 lighthouses, 14 National Historic Landmarks, and 4 national parks.

Attractions and Landmarks

Oregon's sandy beaches are a major tourist attraction. However, there are many other things to do and see in the Beaver State as well.

HISTORIC SITES

Timberline Lodge is located on Mt. Hood. It is North America's only year-round ski area. The lodge was built in just fifteen months between 1936 and 1937. Construction work was done entirely by hand by unemployed craftspeople hired by the Federal Works Project Administration, a former government agency created in 1935 when unemployment was widespread. Inspired by pioneer, Native American, and wildlife themes, local materials were used to create Timberline and its furnishings. The lodge has been carefully restored. In 1978, Timberline was declared a National Historic Landmark.

With its huge wooden beams, rock walls, and scenic views, the lodge is a popular destination for skiers, architecture fans, and nature lovers.

U.S. Highway 101—also known as the Pacific Coast Highway—follows a 363-mile trek along the Oregon coast. Travelers encounter views of the Pacific Ocean, parks, beaches, and lighthouses, including Cape Blanco Light Station near Port Orford. The isolated lighthouse was put into service in 1870. It operated with an oil lantern until 1936 when it was updated with electricity. Visitors to the brick lighthouse may climb the spiral staircase to the top of its 59-foot tower. At the northern end of the highway, travelers cross the 4.1-mile-long

Places to See in Oregon

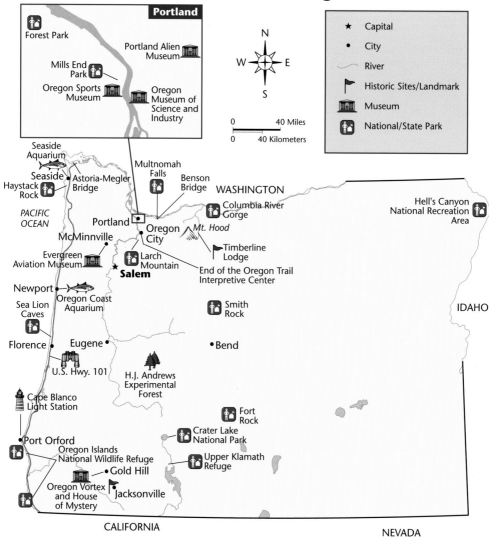

The Nunan House in Jacksonville is also known as the Catalogue House. It was ordered by catalogue in 1892 by merchant Jeremiah Nunan as a Christmas present for his wife Delia. It was shipped in fourteen boxcars from Tennessee and assembled by local workmen at a cost of $7,800.

Astoria-Megler Bridge, where the mouth of the Columbia River gapes wide. The bridge's main span is 1,232 feet in length, the longest continuous truss in the world.

In 1852, gold was discovered in southwestern Oregon. The town of Jacksonville grew along the gold-lined creek beds. It flourished until the late 1870s, when most of the ore was gone. Soon after, Jacksonville became a **ghost town.** The town sprang back to life in the 1960s when residents made a commitment to preserve its 19th-century character. Dozens of cafes, taverns, historic lodgings, museums, antique shops, art galleries, and specialty boutiques now fill the town's original brick and wooden buildings, 80 of which are listed on the National Register of Historic Places. The entire town was designated a National Historic Landmark in 1966.

NATURAL WONDERS

The Upper Klamath Refuge, located in southeastern Oregon, was established in 1928 by President Calvin Coolidge. The **refuge** contains 15,000 acres of mostly freshwater marsh and open water. These environments serve as nesting and brood rearing areas for waterfowl and nesting birds, including American white pelican and several heron species. Bald eagle and osprey nest nearby and can sometimes be seen fishing in refuge waters. Visitors may tour the refuge by boat.

Haystack Rock, at 235 feet high, is the third largest coastal **monolith** in the world. It draws tens of thousands of visitors each year. The huge stand-alone rock is located off the coast of Cannon Beach and is part of the Oregon Islands National Wildlife Refuge. Haystack Rock is protected by its status as a "marine garden." Marine garden is a designation given to natural areas that are heavily visited each year. It means that all living things within the selected area are protected. **Tidepools** around the rock are home to many animals, including limpets, barnacles, starfish, crabs, sea sculpins, and anemones.

Unusually cold weather can turn Multnomah Falls into a frozen icicle with only a few drops reaching the bottom.

Multnomah Falls is located about 30 miles east of Portland in the Columbia River Gorge National Scenic Area. The site is the state's most popular tourist attraction, drawing 2.5 million visitors each year. Multnomah Falls is the second highest year-round waterfall in the nation. Its waters drop 620 feet. The waterfall has two levels: water drops 531 feet from the top of Larch Mountain into a pool and then another 69 feet from the pool to the base of the mountain. Benson Bridge, crafted by Italian stone masons, allows visitors to cross the falls between its upper and lower tiers.

MUSEUMS AND MORE

The Oregon Vortex and House of Mystery near Gold Hill has to be seen to be believed. Here, tennis balls roll uphill and brooms stand on end. Nowhere within the vortex can visitors stand upright. Instead they lean toward **magnetic north.** A *vortex* is the shape of something rotating rapidly. There are many theories about the area's mysterious goings-on. Some say the vortex simply acts as a giant refracting lens, bending light in a circular motion and creating an optical illusion. Others believe it is a place where the earth's **gravitational field** has been distorted.

Map of Oregon

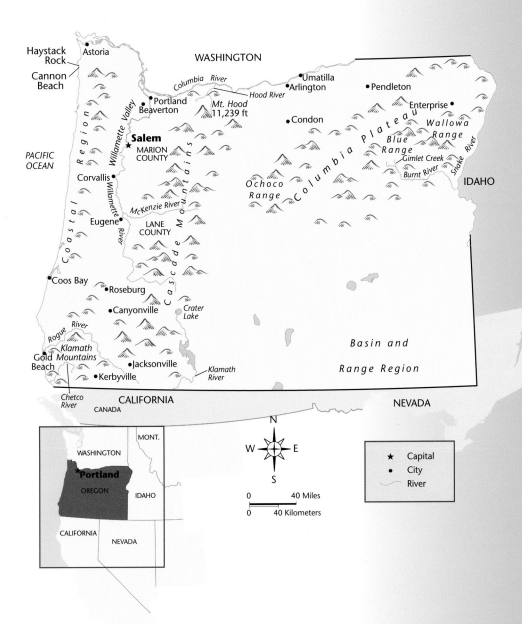

Haystack Rock
Astoria
WASHINGTON
Cannon Beach
Columbia River
Umatilla
Arlington
Pendleton
Hood River
Portland
Beaverton
Enterprise
Mt. Hood 11,239 ft
Condon
Wallowa Range
PACIFIC OCEAN
Salem
MARION COUNTY
Columbia Plateau
Blue Range
Corvallis
Gimlet Creek
Burnt River
Snake River
IDAHO
McKenzie River
Ochoco Range
Eugene
LANE COUNTY
Coos Bay
Roseburg
Canyonville
Crater Lake
Basin and Range Region
Rogue River
Klamath Mountains
Gold Beach
Jacksonville
Klamath River
Kerbyville
Chetco River
CALIFORNIA
NEVADA
CANADA

WASHINGTON
MONT.
Portland
OREGON
IDAHO
CALIFORNIA
NEVADA

N
W E
S

★ Capital
• City
～ River

0   40 Miles
0   40 Kilometers

Glossary

anesthesia   a drug that is given for medical or surgical purposes to reduce feeling to all or part of the body

artifacts   objects remaining from a particular period

bill   a draft of a law presented to a legislature for consideration

canyon   an unusually deep and narrow valley with steep sides

civil   issues that have to do with private rights rather than criminal activity

climate   the general weather conditions of a specific region

constitution   laws determining the basic governing principles of a group and the rights of the individuals

criminal cases   legal action that arises when someone has committed a crime

ecology   a branch of science concerned with the relationships between living things and their environment

elevation   the height of the land measured from sea level

emigrants   people who leave one country to settle in another

entomologist   a person who specializes in the study of insects

environmentalists   those who share a desire to protect the environment and natural resources from overuse, misuse, and pollution

eroded   worn away by water, ice, or wind

fry bread   bread made of flour, baking powder, milk or water and fried in oil, traditional to some Native American peoples

generation   a group of people who are of the same basic age

ghost town   a town deserted because some local natural resource has been used up

gorge   a deep narrow valley with a river running through it

gravitational field   pull of gravity around a specific object

Latino   person of Hispanic heritage (or ancestry), or living in Latin America

lyricist   a person who writes the words for songs

magistrate   a public official authorized to decide questions bought before a court of justice

magnetic north   the northerly direction in the earth's magnetic field toward which a magnetic compass needle points

martyrs   those who sacrifice life or something of great value for a principle or cause

monolith   a large block of stone, often created by erosion from the sea or wind

Nobel Prize   important prizes awarded each year by a Swedish organization that recognizes achievements in various fields

nursery products   plants sold through greenhouses and garden centers

Oregon Country   a region west of the Rocky Mountains and East of the Pacific Ocean that consisted of the land north of 42°N latitude and south of 54°40'N latitude. The area now forms part of the present day Canadian province of British Columbia and the U.S. states of Oregon and Washington

override   to undo an earlier action by another person or group

pictographs   pictures representing words or ideas

plywood   a strong board made by gluing thin sheets of wood together under heat and pressure

Pulitzer Prize   one of a group of prizes awarded each year for works of journalism, history, and biography

recall   the legal removal of elected or appointed public officials from office

refuge   a place that provides shelter or protection

sickle-cell anemia   disease caused by abnormal red blood cells that results in low energy, harm to human blood vessels and organs, and other effects

tidepools   shallow pools of water that remain when the tide goes out

tributaries   streams that flow into larger streams or rivers

vetoes   rejects, as in a governor's or president's right to refuse to pass a law

volcanoes   vents in the earth's crust from which melted or hot rock and steam come out

More Books to Read

Joseph, Paul. *Oregon.* Edina, Minn.: Abdo & Daughters, 1998.

Kimmel, Elizabeth Cody. *As Far as the Eye Can Reach: Lewis and Clark's Westward Quest.* New York, New York: Random House, 2003.

Shannon, Terry Miller. *Oregon (From Sea to Shining Sea).* New York, New York: Children's Press, 2003.

Oregon (One Nation). Mankato, Minn.: Capstone Press, 2003.

Peters, Stephanie True. *A Kid's Guide to Drawing America: How to Draw Oregon's Sights and Symbols.* New York, New York: Rosen Publishing Group's PowerKids Press, 2002.

Index

About the Author

Mary Boone lives in the Northwest and writes for *People, Teen People,* and *Seattle Homes and Lifestyles.* She loves Portland and has run the Portland Marathon twice. Mary recommends everyone put Multnomah Falls on their list of places to visit.